Am I Crazy?

The Most Often Asked Question in Therapy

Amanda Brewer, B. Beh Sc (Phych).

BALBOA.
PRESS

A DIVISION OF HAY HOUSE

Balboa Press books may be ordered through booksellers or by contacting:

Balboa Press
A Division of Hay House
1663 Liberty Drive
Bloomington, IN 47403
www.balboapress.com.au
1 (877) 407-4847

Because of the dynamic nature of the Internet, any web addresses or links contained in this book may have changed since publication and may no longer be valid. The views expressed in this work are solely those of the author and do not necessarily reflect the views of the publisher, and the publisher hereby disclaims any responsibility for them.

The author of this book does not dispense medical advice or prescribe the use of any technique as a form of treatment for physical, emotional, or medical problems without the advice of a physician, either directly or indirectly. The intent of the author is only to offer information of a general nature to help you in your quest for emotional and spiritual well-being. In the event you use any of the information in this book for yourself, which is your constitutional right, the author and the publisher assume no responsibility for your actions.

Print information available on the last page.

ISBN: 978-1-5043-1670-5 (sc)
ISBN: 978-1-5043-1793-1 (e)

Balboa Press rev. date: 05/21/2019

To my wonderful husband, Robbie, who has always believed in me and supported everything I have wanted to do. My good friend Elizabeth, who has been my rock forever. Terry, my wonderful cousin, who proofread and edited this book and many of my uni assignments. And lastly, my children, children-in-law, and grandchildren. You are the reasons for everything I do. If I can do it, so can you.

Introduction

"Am I crazy?" "What's wrong with me?" These are questions I've been asked many times. It takes enormous courage firstly to admit to yourself that you need help and then to make an appointment. Sometimes it is even harder to attend that appointment. I have had many clients who confessed at the end of their first appointment that they almost didn't make it.

This book, therefore, is for all the brave, vulnerable, anxious people who would like to feel better about themselves and enjoy a better quality of life. The information is taken from what I have learned and shared with my clients along with techniques, helpful practices, and information I have gained from others. Wherever I share others' research or findings, they are acknowledged.

Chapter 1

Anger

It has often been said to me by clients, "I can't control my anger, and it hurts the people I love." Out-of-control anger is out-of-control fear or anxiety. Everyone has some anxiety. If it weren't for anxiety, you would forget to look before you crossed the road. If you imagine your anxiety score as rating between 0 and 100, then 10 would likely be the lowest you would be—unless you're dead or in a coma. In moderation, anxiety is good as it helps protect us from harm. If you're crossing the road and a bus is coming towards you, you don't have to stop and think, *What should I do?* Chemicals in your brain react in a split second, your "flight/fight/freeze" instinct triggers, and you hopefully get out of the way. However, some people who have had a lot of trauma in their past freeze at additional times of perceived danger.

Anxiety is an instinct that humans and animals share, but humans are the only species that tries to ignore, push away, or disregard the feeling. If an animal thinks something in the bush is going to attack it, nothing will make it go near the bush. People will go and check, just in case they're wrong. We don't listen to—or believe—our instincts. I encourage clients to listen to their instincts and believe in themselves.

Our brains are powerful, and we always believe the brain works in one's best interest. But sometimes the processes become a little crazy—not *us* but the processes in our brain. It has been proven by MRI machines in many research studies that the amygdala, an almond-shaped part of the brain towards the back, controls and releases stress chemicals when we think that we may be in some danger—real or imagined. (See the end of the book for resources, or visit my website: freemindspsychology.com.au).

A major problem is that the physical evolution of the human brain hasn't kept pace with the evolution of our environment. Cognitive researchers believe that the perception of danger causes a chemical change in the brain, which sends signals to the body to prepare to escape or fight. These bodily changes cause the stress or anxiety symptoms, such as increased heart rate; shallow, faster breathing; and shutting down of processes that aren't necessary in times of stress.

The fact that our brains haven't evolved much in thousands of years means that the chemical signal for, "Help, a lion is chasing me! I'm about to die!" is the same as, "I just opened a huge bill I didn't budget for. I'm in trouble!" It's just the volume of chemicals that is different.

But why do some people cope while others fall apart? The answer has to do with our experiences and coping skills. Our brains have a protective system called a *set point* that works to keep us safe by bringing levels of chemicals that have risen abnormally high back down to the baseline. If you think of the range of these chemicals as going from zero to a hundred, no one is ever at zero. Baseline is about ten. As stated previously, we need some anxiety.

The trouble for some people is that they have had traumatic events in their lives, as we all have. Traumatic experiences, abusive experiences, or abusive interactions are in this book defined as, "any interaction that is less than nurturing." People react to situations or interactions differently, depending on their experiences and their beliefs about themselves and the world. No one can tell us how we should feel or react to anything. Each person's experiences are unique to him or her.

In today's world, the trauma or upset that causes elevated levels of stress hormones doesn't immediately decrease. Depending on the cause, it could take weeks or months. This can result in a resetting of the set point, perhaps to forty or fifty, depending on what is happening. And you stay there because the stress has gone on for so long. Research cited by neuroscientist Dr. Sara Lazar in her TEDx talk on meditation and how it can change brain structure, found that stress enlarges the amygdala, which stays enlarged unless you do something to reverse it. As time goes on and you experience more stressors, your resting set point has crept up to ninety, even though you think you're calm. (The web address is in the Resources section.)

Once this happens, even an upset such as, "I can't find my car keys," or, "Someone's given me a strange look," is enough to send our stress levels up to one hundred. For the amygdala, one hundred means "Panic stations! Serious danger! Something bad is happening!" The flight/fight response is activated, and we react by screaming, crying, shutting down, running away, or doing other extreme responses, which later, when we have calmed down, seem like an overreaction. This explains why we can have meltdowns even when we want to be calm, and then we beat ourselves up later for reacting the way we did.

If anxiety extends for too long, it can also cause physical problems. A physical result of stress is that it causes blood that is not absolutely necessary to keep our internal organs functioning to be sent to the muscles needed for the flight/fight/freeze response. This has the effect of shutting down the digestive system so that we don't feel hungry. If we don't eat for a while or miss too many meals, our brains start to complain. The brain uses about 80 percent of the glucose in the body to keep it functioning, so it sends the message, "I need sugar." We then tend to grab something that quickly turns into sugar in our body, such as bread, biscuits, or junk food. Then our brains relax for a moment because they've been fed. But because these foods are so addictive, we don't just eat the right amount; we eat the whole packet. When the brain becomes overloaded with sugar, it tries to compensate by creating extra insulin. The insulin copes so well that we end up feeling like we need more sugar. This can be the start of insulin resistance, which can be the precursor to diabetes. I usually suggest to clients that if they find this is happening, they should eat some sort of protein instead of carbohydrate as protein gets absorbed slowly. It stops the cycle of sugar spikes and lows.

The good news is there are processes that can change brain chemistry so we can better cope with stress and anxiety and rewire our brains.

Chapter 2

Self-Esteem

I have found one of the fastest ways to combat both depression and anxiety is to build one's self-esteem. From time to time, well-meaning people in our lives have criticized us, thinking they are making us stronger, better, or more resilient. I have talked to many parents from all walks of life and haven't yet met any whose thought process was *How can I mess up my child? I know. I'll do or say …* They are all doing the best they can with the knowledge, skills, and experiences they have at that time. Unfortunately, we often take whatever was said to heart and make it part of our inner self-talk, mistakenly believing the harder we are on ourselves, the more disciplined we will be, and the better we will do in our lives. In my experience, the opposite is true. The harder we are on ourselves, the worse we feel, and the more we just want to go to bed and pull the blankets over our heads.

A few years ago, I discovered a PDF by Louise L. Hay that I find to be very useful. The following quote explains her experience and belief, which I have also found to be true with my clients.

I have found that there is only one thing that heals every problem, and that is: *to love yourself.* When people start to love themselves more each day, it's amazing how their lives get better. They feel better. They get the jobs they want. They have the money they need. Their relationships either improve, or the negative one's dissolve and new ones begin. Loving yourself is a wonderful adventure; it's like learning to fly. Imagine if we all had the power to fly at will? How exciting it would be! Let's begin to love ourselves now.

The Twelve Commandments to Help You Learn How to Love Yourself

I've given you the headings. For the full article, go to her website.

1. Stop all criticism.
2. Forgive yourself.
3. Don't scare yourself.
4. Be gentle, kind, and patient.
5. Be kind to your mind.
6. Praise yourself.
7. Support yourself.
8. Be loving to your negatives.
9. Take care of your body.
10. Do mirror work.
11. Love yourself. Do it now.
12. Have fun.

The web address is in the Resources section.

Learning to love ourselves not only makes a huge difference to our relationship with ourselves but also to all our other relationships. As our self-esteem increases, we accept less bad behaviour from others, and people naturally start treating us better. Some of these suggestions are hard to start with; however, I have done them, and they work. I know others who have found they work as well.

Dr. Sara Lazar's TEDx talk, "How Meditation Changes the Brain," relates to her research on meditation. This research found that meditation builds self-esteem, creates more contentment in life, reduces depression and anxiety, and helps relieve insomnia and pain. Anything we do repeatedly creates changes in the brain. This is called neuroplasticity. Neuroplasticity rewires the brain by changing neural pathways. The more we repeat a thought, the thicker and stronger that neural pathway becomes. If we start thinking a thought less often, that pathway becomes thinner and can disappear completely over time. Meditation makes healthier neural pathways across the two sides of the brain. There is much evidence that meditation can reduce anxiety, depression, pain, and insomnia. The web address is in the Resources section.

Dr. Shawn Achor's TEDx talk, "The Happiness Advantage: Linking Positive Brains to Performance," relates to his research on happiness and how it effects the brain. He also cites meditation as one of the practices that can create happiness. The web address is in the Resources section.

You will notice meditation will come up again and again in the research I mention in these pages. There are many kinds of meditation. Mindfulness meditation means you meditate by yourself, closing your eyes, slowing your breathing, and allowing your thoughts to just flow through, or by being conscious of the present moment. This form of meditation can be difficult, especially if you have a very busy mind, but is a great practice if you master it. A slightly easier option is to listen to a guided meditation, available on apps, YouTube, or CDs found at markets or health or well-being shops.

Amanda Brewer, B. Beh Sc (Phych).

A third method, which I and people I've recommended it to have found useful is binaural beat meditation, which is claimed to change the neural pathways in our brain. Resources can also be found in the same way as those for guided meditation.

Chapter 3

Overall Health and Well-Being

We have all heard the saying, "Healthy mind, healthy body." The two are interchangeable. The mind affects the body, and the body affects the mind. It's called metaphysics. There has been extensive research done in this field for many years; a Google search reveals many articles on this subject. This chapter covers mostly a relatively new theory on one of the causes of chronic depression and anxiety.

We all have neurons in our brains. They are the nerve cells that transmit messages from one part of the brain to another. If the neurons are healthy and working well, our thought processes and emotions are healthier as well. Recently, it was found that we also have neurons in our gut, and the health of these neurons depends on the correct balance of good and bad gut bacteria. A major factor that influences this balance is diet—especially the amounts of sugar, alcohol, and toxins we ingest—and the amount of processed food we eat. Processed foods and sugar reduce good bacteria and feed bad bacteria.

Another factor is how much stress we have in our lives and our coping skills. It's not how much stress we have, but how we handle it and whether we are able to see stress as a threat or a challenge. Everybody has some stress and anxiety. The only people who are never stressed are already in the cemetery. Without any anxiety, you would forget to look out for danger. The only difference is some people cope better than others. Calmness flows in others. Or to put it another way, stress breeds more stress in ourselves and others.

Dr. Daniel Amen is a psychiatrist who has conducted much research on the brain and how it affects mental health. He believes that when our brains and guts are in optimal working order, depression and anxiety may improve or disappear.

I'm not talking about situational depression or anxiety. If there is a traumatic circumstance in your life, for example if you have just experienced a loss, you are supposed to feel sad and stressed (grief manifests as stress in our body). It's part of grief and the healing process. I'm talking about long-standing problems that have caused changes in the way we cope with things and are resistant to change. Following is what Dr. Amen has concluded. For a complete version, the Web address is in the Resources section.

His research states that the brain is the most amazing organ in the body. It controls one's ability to learn, love, and behave in a positive, productive way that enables us to have enriching personal relationships. When our brains, or our family's brains function correctly, the family's experiences tend to be positive and effective. When our brains or the brain of one or more family members is troubled, the family experiences increased stress and strain.

He states in his article that our brains is very complex. It is only about 2 percent of your body's weight, yet it uses approximately 20 to 30 percent of the calories you consume, 20 percent of the oxygen you breathe, and 25 percent of the blood flow in your body. And your brain is about 85 percent water! It has about 100 billion nerve cells and more connections (synapses) in it than there are stars in the universe.

A piece of brain tissue the size of a grain of sand contains approximately 100,000 neurons and 1 billion synapses. If you don't take care of your brain, you lose on average 85,000 brain cells a day. That is what causes brain ageing. However, with care and time, you can reverse that trend and dramatically slow the ageing process and increase your mental agility.

Finding out how to care for your brain, and the brains of your family, is the first and most important step to success. When the brain works well, you (and your family) work well. Dr. Amen's research found that these things help repair your brain.

Love Your Brain: When he first started taking SPECT scans at around age thirty-seven, he took a scan of his own brain and was surprised at how unhealthy it looked. After learning more about how to improve brain health, he practiced what he preached. A scan some years later showed his brain health had improved. Some of the changes he implemented were more good-quality sleep, less junk food and soft drinks, and a healthier diet overall. Loving your brain is the first step towards creating a brain-healthy life.

Increase the Brain's Reserve: After looking at tens of thousands of scans, he developed a concept he called "brain reserve." This is the cushion of healthy brain tissue we have to use when unexpected stress comes our way. This may explain why some people cope with lots of drama and trauma while others can't cope with issues that others would think were minor. Amen believes the more reserves we have, the more resilient we are in times of trouble. The less reserves, the more vulnerable we are. He found in his practice that people who had brain injuries did not cope as well as those with healthier brains.

He also found factors that can decrease brain reserves include whether your mother smoked, drank alcohol, or was under constant stress when she was pregnant with you.

The good news is that you can work on increasing your brain reserve. For example, we know that chronic stress kills cells in the memory centre of the brain. Therefore, try to stay away from drugs, excess alcohol, negative thinking, a fast-food diet, environmental toxins, and anything that decreases blood flow to the brain—such as lack of sleep, untreated sleep apnoea, smoking, or too much caffeine. (I know, I'm a killjoy.)

Protect Your Brain: Simply put, your brain is soft, and your skull is hard. So wear your seat belt, drive in safe vehicles, don't hit balls with your head, and stay off the roof. Dr. Amen found in his practice that one of the most common causes of brain injuries in men over forty was falling off the roof.

Stop Poisoning Your Brain: Avoid alcohol and illegal drugs, artificial sweeteners, limit your caffeine intake, and don't use cleaning products without proper ventilation.

Protect Your Memory: Take early memory problems seriously, and don't just dismiss them as a normal part of ageing. According to a UCLA study, quoted by Dr. Amen, many older people with Alzheimer's disease are not diagnosed until they are in the moderate to severe stages of the disorder, when not much can be done to help them. He believes people should be screened yearly after the age of fifty for memory problems, using simple paper-and-pencil tests. He has one on the website, mybrainfitlife.com. One of the most important things you can do to keep your memory strong is exercise, for example, walking.

Good Sleep Is Good for Brain Health: Many people have trouble sleeping. This affects their moods, memory, and ability to concentrate. Dr. Amen recommends that you eliminate anything that might interfere with sleep, such as caffeine, alcohol, reading scary books, or electronic screen time before bedtime. He recommends trying natural supplements, such as melatonin, valerian, kava, or 5-HTP. Hypnosis and meditation can help, and they are also very good for the relief of pain, anxiety, and depression.

Learn Brain-Healthy Ways to Deal with Pain: Pain is one of the most debilitating symptoms that we can have. Chronic pain negatively affects everything—sleep, mood, memory, and concentration. Scans Dr. Amen conducted showed that the use of chronic pain medications may be harmful to brain function. Long-term use of pain medications makes the brain look like those of people who regularly drink too much.

I would never suggest that you throw out your pain medications. I know some people would rather die than live with pain, and pain itself can contribute to depression. I know I feel down when the pain in my knees flares up. Because of what Dr. Amen has seen on these scans, he developed an interest in alternative treatments for pain. Fish oil, acupuncture, music therapy, hypnosis, and meditation all have scientific evidence that they may be helpful.

He also learned that pain and depression tend to go hand in hand. It is proven that for some people, using natural supplements can help both problems. SAMe or the antidepressant medicine Cymbalta are the ones he recommends.

There are many natural ways to help the brain. Of course, you should talk to your doctor. If your medical professionals are not knowledgeable about natural supplements, as many were never taught about them in medical school, a naturopath may be helpful.

Also, try eliminating all artificial sweeteners from your diet. There is anecdotal evidence that these can increase pain. I had some chewing gum a while ago, which was unusual for me. I woke up the next morning and could barely move. I couldn't work out why until I read the gum packet. It contained aspartame, which I had worked out previously affected me adversely. I threw the remainder away. I don't think artificial sweeteners affect everyone. However, if you hurt, it may be something to consider.

A Brain-Healthy Diet: Eat lean protein, such as turkey or chicken. Include low-glycaemic, high-fibre carbohydrates. These are carbohydrates high in fibre that do not raise your blood sugar and include such as whole grains and green, leafy vegetables. Healthy fats that contain omega three fatty acids are healthier for the brain. They are found in foods such as tuna, salmon, avocados, and walnuts.

Since the brain is mostly water, anything that dehydrates you is bad for the brain. This includes alcohol, caffeine, excess salt, or not drinking enough fluids. So drink plenty of water to keep yourself well hydrated.

Physical Exercise: Exercise boosts blood flow to the brain. Plus, it increases chemicals that are important for learning, memory, and stimulating the growth of new brain cells. Dr. Amen states that thirty minutes three or four times a week is all you need. If you don't know what else to do, take a brisk walk, as though you're late to be somewhere.

Mental Exercise: Once you exercise and boost blood flow to your brain, the next step is mental exercise. Dr. Amen found in one of his studies using lab rats that exercise generated new cells in the learning and memory centres of the brain. These new cells lasted about four weeks. If they were not stimulated by new learning, the new cells died. This is neuroplasticity in action. There is a saying in scientific circles, "Neurons that fire together wire together."

Dr. Amen has a lot more information and mental tests you can do on his website.

Notice What you Love about Your Life and Other People Instead of What You Don't: Basically, this is noticing the things you are grateful for instead of focusing on the negatives. You will notice that gratitude is also mentioned many times in the research I quote. Amen talks about a study he conducted with psychologist Noelle Nelson on the power of appreciation. He scanned her twice, once when she was focused on what she loved about her life and again while she focused on what she hated about her life. The scans were radically different. The first scan looked healthy, while the second showed decreased activity in several important areas of her brain.

Be a positive light in people's lives. Focus on what you love about the meaningful people in your life, and try to be a guiding force for them. Again, this is gratitude and appreciation.

Another theory that is being researched ties in with Amen's recommendation to take probiotics for gut health. It has been known for some time that neurons, the cells usually found in the brain, can also be found in other organs of the body, including the gut.

Dr. Scott Bay found in his research that the most promising finding to emerge from recent microbiome research is the possibility that probiotics can alleviate symptoms of depression and other mood disorders. Many researchers in this area believe that the gut is the second brain. Following is a summary of some research that he quotes in an article. The web address is in the Resource section of this book, or for a direct link, go to my website.

Amanda Brewer, B. Beh Sc (Phych).

Do Probiotics Have a First-Line Role in Depression Treatment?

Bay states in an interview that "I absolutely envision a time when probiotic/prebiotic therapies will become first line interventions for psychiatric illnesses. The research indicates things are headed that way and I look forward to the time when we reach that point."

He has worked with adults who have anxiety, depression, bipolar disorder, ADHD, and other psychiatric disorders. He uses conventional drugs but always within a comprehensive wholistic strategy that includes psychotherapy, exercise, and good nutrition.

Over the years, Bay has incorporated natural supplements such as Deplin (a prescription version of l-methylfolate), a form of folate found naturally in the body; SAM-e, a natural anti-anxiety medication; and vitamin D for depression; and Vayarin (omega-3) for ADHD. More recently, he began introducing probiotics to his patients. "Clinically, I have always observed strong correlations between psychiatric illnesses and gastrointestinal symptoms. Patients with Depression and especially Anxiety have worse symptoms of irritable bowel syndrome (IBS), GERD, hiatal hernia, Crohn's Disease, and ulcerative colitis. When the Depression and Anxiety were under control, GI symptoms either were much less or resolved.

"The explosion of recent knowledge about the gut microbiome seems to me to be the way to explain the linkage between brain and gut symptoms, and to open doors to new treatments."

For Bay, the interest began with a 2015 triple-blind study from the Leiden University Institute for Psychological Research in Holland, showing that a multispecies combination of bifidobacterium and lactobacillus strains could lower cognitive reactivity to sad moods, a marker for susceptibility to depression. The study found that this combination of probiotics reduced cognitive reactivity.

The research investigators randomized forty people to either an inert placebo or a probiotic. They assessed mood states and cognitive reactivity before and after the four-week intervention using the standardized Leiden Index of Depression sensitivity. Participants received once-daily sachets containing a dry powder; the controls got an inert mix of maize starch and maltodextrin, while the active treatment group got the same carrier but containing a powdered probiotic. The product was taken by mixing it with lukewarm milk.

It was found that after four weeks, the probiotic-treated subjects showed notable changes on several parameters of the Leiden Index. Aggression dropped from a pre-intervention mean of 8.7 to 6.25, risk aversion went from 10.0 to 7.95, and rumination (the focused attention on the symptoms of one's distress and on its possible causes and consequences, as opposed to its solutions) went from 11.2 to 8.25. No similar changes were recorded in the control group. The study also showed the probiotic group showed less cognitive reactivity to low mood states. (Better mood)

My belief is that current work by many eminent researchers shows that the quality of food intake affects our bodies and that the mind/body connection is very important.

Chapter 4

Giving, Receiving, and Gratitude

Dr. Shawn Achor's TEDx talk on how happiness practices can rewire the brain includes as one of the practices random acts of kindness. Much research shows that being altruistic (choosing to do things for others just for the joy of it) helps us as much as it does the person we are helping.

This brings me to another topic that many people have trouble with: how to be on the receiving end of acts of kindness. Most people like to think of themselves as being good people; that is, those who help other people. However, we often have more trouble being on the receiving end. In my practice, I have been amazed at how many wonderful, caring people don't feel worthy of receiving help, compliments, or gifts.

My argument to them is yes, it is good to give, and it makes us feel better. However, if everyone wants to give, then who is receiving? It is also an act of service to be on the receiving end for a change. For example, if a child has made a gift for you and is excited about giving it to you, you accept it because you don't want to upset the child. We don't say, "Thank you, but I already have five finger paintings." I have seen and heard of many adults who are feeling overwhelmed and needing help, but when people offer help, they say, "No, it's fine. I can manage." This denies the other person the pleasure of helping. It actually takes a person of higher self-esteem and sense of self to accept help.

One way to build your sense of self and build self-esteem and self-worth is a gratitude practice.

One practice recommended by Dr. Shawn Achor in his TEDx talk is to write down three new things that you're grateful for every day for twenty-one days. I find it a good practice to do with loved ones, either before sleep or at the dinner table, with each person saying three things they are grateful for. This practice trains our brains to look at things we're happy about instead of all the things we feel are wrong. I love the following quote from Oprah Winfrey, who has for many years been an advocate of gratitude practice: "Be thankful for what you have; you'll end up having more. If you concentrate on what you don't have, you will never, ever have enough."

It has been shown many times that the daily habits of gratitude and appreciation confer one of the highest emotional states you can experience. When you cultivate gratitude, you are able to feel true joy and contentment, no matter what you have or don't have in your life.

However, many people find that it requires great diligence to cultivate a persistent attitude of appreciation. That's because we've been culturally conditioned to focus on what we don't have rather than appreciating what we've already received or achieved. To help you combat this conditioning, following isthe "6 Daily Habits of Gratitude that Will Attract More Abundance and Joy" from the website of Jack Canfield, author of *Chicken Soup for the Soul* and

The Success Principles: How to Get From Where You Are to Where You Want to Be which I have shared with many clients who have found it as helpful as I have in my own life. The web address is in the Resources section. On his website, it states that people can share his work if they include this statement:

> Jack Canfield, America's #1 Success Coach, is founder of the billion-dollar book brand *Chicken Soup for the Soul*® and a leading authority on Peak Performance and Life Success. If you're ready to jump-start your life, make more money, and have more fun and joy in all that you do, get FREE success tips from Jack Canfield now at: www.FreeSuccessStrategies.com

1. Take seven minutes each morning to write down everything you appreciate in life.

Starting your day this way helps you set your mind to be receptive and grateful for everything the day will bring. It also helps you cultivate an air of positivity that makes you naturally more attractive to other positive people—and inspires them to want to help you achieve your goals.

2. Make a conscious effort to appreciate at least three people every day.

By letting people know how much you appreciate them, you increase their own senses of appreciation and self-worth, and encourage them to pay this positive energy forward to other people. While most people enjoy receiving verbal appreciation, written notes are also nice as they can be saved and reread. A friend's husband used to leave little notes in their sugar basin so she would find them when she made her first cup of coffee for the morning. This practice of random acts of kindness is also endorsed by Dr. Shawn Achor's research. He found that it also helped the giver to feel happier and have better self-esteem.

3. Play the appreciation game (like the Glad game from *Pollyanna* if you're old enough to remember).

Set a specific time each day to consciously appreciate everything you encounter. An ideal time to do this is on your way to or from work. Appreciate the people you pass, the road you walk down, the cars that let you merge into a different lane.

Look for the good in all situations, even those you would normally view as negative. For example, when Jack Canfield's wife was in a car accident, she could have chosen to berate herself or question her judgement. Instead, she focused on her gratitude for suffering only minor injuries and for the help she received from other drivers.

4. Carry a physical token of gratitude in your pocket.

A suggestion I have heard from a few sources is to carry a physical token of gratitude, such as a heart-shaped stone, crystal, or some other small item in your pocket. This physical reminder can bring you back to your daily habit of gratitude when your mind has drifted elsewhere. This practice suggests that when you reach into your pocket throughout the day and feel the token, use it as a reminder to stop, breathe, and take a moment to fully experience the emotion of gratitude.

5. Remember to appreciate the smallest blessings.

The best way to activate your gratitude is by acknowledging the gifts most people take for granted. If you have food in your refrigerator, clothes in your wardrobe, and a roof over your head, you are better off than 75 percent of the world's population.

If you eat three meals a day, you are far better off than the one billion people on the planet who eat once a day at most. Do you have clean water to drink? Is your family healthy? Do you have a phone? How about a car that allows you to travel to work or to explore the country? Do you have a computer and internet access to stay in touch with the world, get access to education, and possibly use for work for which you are paid? These daily conveniences are gifts that most people in the world do not enjoy.

6. Appreciate yourself.

Last but not least, don't forget to appreciate your own positive qualities and accomplishments. In addition to celebrating your big successes, acknowledge your small daily successes as well. We all need acknowledgment, but the most important acknowledgment is that which we give ourselves. Marisa Peer, an English psychologist who has done a number of talks for YouTube, including a TEDx talk, states in her talks that self-praise is more beneficial than other people praising us as they may have agendas or ulterior motives.

It may not feel natural at first to focus on appreciating what you already have, but it does help. It may sound daunting, but the more you do it, the easier it becomes.

If all this seems too much for you at the moment, you can start smaller. Dr. Shawn Achor's research suggests that just writing down three new things that you could be grateful for every day for twenty-one days in a row is enough to rewire your brain into looking for the positives instead of the negatives. As I have mentioned before, I often recommend doing it as a family exercise, going around the family at the dinner table or in the car on the way home at the end of the day, with each family member stating three things they were grateful for that day. It can bring the family closer together and help all family members to be more positive.

Chapter 5

I Am Enough

We are all enough all the time! British psychologist Marisa Peer believes the problem of not feeling enough is a worldwide problem and, "the biggest disease affecting humanity." She has TEDx talks and other clips on YouTube if you are interested in further research on this topic. Dr Brene Brown also talks about believing "we are enough" is essential for being a "whole hearted person" in her TEDx talk on the power of vulnerability.

Dr. Robert Holden, in his book *Shift Happens*, relates the story of a woman who brought her newborn to one of his talks. He noticed that people were being distracted by the baby, so he included the baby in the talk. He encouraged people to think of the baby and then themselves as babies. A baby is born innocent, perfect, and believing that he or she is worthy. We still have that baby inside us. The only things that have changed are our beliefs and our negative self-talk which tells us we are not good enough.

In Dr Brown's talk, mentioned above, she talks about her research into worthiness. She found the only difference between people who believe they are worthy and those who don't is that the people who felt they were, believed they were. That was the *only* difference. We have a choice; we can always change our beliefs.

Society has a lot to answer for. TV, magazines, and media in general are all telling us subliminally that we would be better with this hair product, that car, a house by the water, and so on. Marisa Peer also has a number of very good talks available as YouTube clips that are helpful in aiding us to feel better about ourselves.

I have found in my own practice that as clients' self-esteem improves, everything in their lives magically improves. (See Louise L. Hays, *12 Ways to Love Yourself* from chapter 2.)

Another issue, which I touched on earlier, that I have found affects our moods, self-esteem, the way that we see ourselves, and the way we perceive how others see us is chronic pain. It can also affect whether we feel good enough, especially if because of pain or fatigue we can't do what other people can do easily and simply.

Dr. John E. Sarno wrote a number of books on a syndrome he called tension myositis syndrome (TMS). He believed that the people coming to see him had genuine physical pain that also contained an emotional component, and if they dealt with the emotional component, their physical pain subsided. I have found this to be true in my life. I have managed juvenile rheumatoid arthritis since I was fourteen, and I know beyond a shadow of a doubt that it has been worse at times of my life that were highly stressful and highly emotional (while I am writing this, I am fifty-five). Here are some suggestions I have used from a TMS help forum. I shared them with some of my clients, and they also found them helpful. The web address is in the Resources section.

> Acceptance—Check first that doctors haven't found any physical reasons for the pain.

Journaling—Journaling helps us get in touch with our emotions that could be causing physical pain.

Meditation (again)—Set aside ten minutes a day for meditation. It may take some time to discover what time works best for you. I find my mind is less busy first thing in the morning. During the day, you can also do mindfulness mediation. One of my clients found an app which sounded a Tibetan bell at regular intervals to remind her to do her mindfulness minute. This, allied with deep breathing, can be very relaxing. Search the internet for 4/7/8 breathing.

Targets or goals—Set goals for yourself, both small and large. The writer of this piece found that his pain was partially generated by his previous experience; an activity appears to cause pain, so the next time you attempt that activity, your stress levels rise, heightening pain awareness and worsening the pain experienced. This conditioned fear response can only be overcome by setting small-term goals to recondition yourself to activities without pain.

Visualisation—Adopt visualisation techniques. Olympic athletes use visualisation techniques to improve their performances. Imagining doing activities that cause pain without pain helps reduce the conditioned pain response. It can also help you better perform simple tasks if you visualise them positively first.

Positive attitude—Write yourself several positive affirmations or positive sayings. For example:

"TMS is real, but the pain is just emotional."

"It is okay to not succeed in everything I do."

"The pain is just caused by a lack of oxygenated blood; there is no long-term damage."

Oxygenated stress can be lessened by meditation and other breathing exercises. I have found that saying these affirmations to myself whenever I feel an onset of pain helps.

Exercise—Start exercising. As mentioned before, this will make you feel better and get your blood flowing, which oxygenates the muscles. You should notice that your pain diminishes with time. Mine did.

Commitment—Take things slowly, and give yourself at least a month of genuine application. Ask yourself how much you would be prepared to pay to be cured of your chronic pain. If you're anything like me, it would be every penny you could afford. Ultimately, there is nothing to lose. If after a month you're no better off, well, you've given it a go. If it works, then you have your life back.

Not getting disheartened—The author of these suggestions found in his experience that some people reported an almost immediate reduction in pain symptoms after adopting TMS techniques. For others, it seemed to be a longer process. The important thing is to not get disheartened if you don't notice overnight changes. For some of the success stories on his forum it was a journey that took many months. If you are struggling, it may be wise to speak to a medical professional who accepts the TMS concept. He or she might be able to point you in the right direction.

Another way to deal with negative self-beliefs and even pain that I used and found worked for emotional and physical pain is an energy healing technique called emotional freedom technique (EFT). A counsellor named Gary Craig developed this technique which I describe as similar to acupuncture except it is acupressure. No needles involved. It's also sometimes called tapping because people tap with their fingers on specific acupuncture points using just the pressure of their fingertips.

The ancient Chinese, who used acupuncture around three thousand years ago, believed out bodies have energy pathways which they named meridians. They believed that any intense pain or emotions was blocked energy in these pathways, and if you knew where the pathway was closest to the surface and activated it in some way, the blockage would clear. Energy could then start flowing again, causing the pain or emotion to dissipate.

Below is a handout that I compiled for my clients explaining how to use this technique. Anyone can do it for themselves by themselves. Or if you prefer, there are many YouTube videos that you can watch and participate with on many different emotional subjects.

The Basic Recipe

1. Where in your body do you feel the emotional issue most strongly?

2. Determine the distress level on a scale of 0–10, where 10 is maximum intensity, and 0 is no intensity:

    10, 9, 8, 7, 6, 5, 4, 3, 2, 1, 0

3. The Setup: Repeat this statement three times while continuously tapping the karate chop point on the side of the hand (large dot on hand diagram below).

Even though I have _____ (name the problem), I deeply and completely love and accept myself.

4. The Tapping Sequence: Tap about seven times on each of the energy points in these two diagrams while repeating a brief phrase that reminds you of the problem.

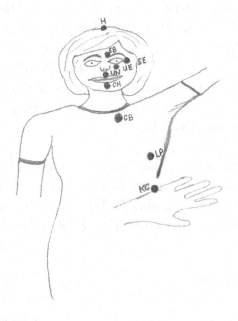

5. Determine your distress level again also on a scale of 0–10. If it's still high, say,

Even though I have some remaining _____ (problem), I deeply and completely love and accept myself.

6. Repeat from step 1 till your distress level is as close to 0 as possible.

I have used EFT for many years and found it useful also in moments of stress. For example, one day long ago, I was having an argument with one of my then teenage daughters. It wasn't going well, and we were both getting to the illogical stage. I took a breath and took myself away to the bathroom. I spent a few minutes tapping on feeling angry. I was then able to calm down enough to go back and have a calm, constructive, discussion.

When I first learnt about EFT, I used to do about twenty minutes every night before I went to sleep, concentrating on old issues, angers, and hurts I'd held on to from as far back as childhood. I found to my surprise that as I dissipated old emotions, I felt better and freer in the present. I highly recommend web searching EFT and watching some YouTube clips, or going to www.thetappingsolution. com to learn more.

Chapter 6

Breath of Life

Many people today do not use the whole of their diaphragm or lungs when they breathe. We spend a lot of time sitting and more time moving slowly. In days gone by, most people did some physical labour in their jobs. This shallow breathing can cause physical problems in our bodies, including the build up of toxins or inflammation.

Wim Hof got his nickname "The Iceman" after he broke several records resisting the effects of cold temperatures. He seems to have found a way of using controlled breathing in cold temperatures to influence his mind and body to behave in a more effective way. He uses his mind to control his body. Some of his feats include climbing Mount Kilimanjaro in shorts, running a half marathon above the Arctic Circle in his bare feet, and standing in a container while covered with ice cubes for more than 112 minutes.

Hof believes that all us can do the same exceptional things his body allows him to do, including improve our depression and anxiety. Therefore, he has developed his Wim Hof method (WHM) that gives ordinary people the tools to take control of their bodies. Hof's motto is, "What I am capable of, everybody can learn." Using his method, he teaches people from all over the world to control their bodies and achieve extraordinary things. Feeling in control of yourself helps to make you feel empowered and improves your self-esteem.

His method is basically a three-step process of breathing techniques, cold therapy (teaching your body how to manage different experiences of cold temperatures), and forms of exercise and meditation.

Over the years, Hof has drawn the curiosity of several scientists. They have subjected him, and even some of his students, to various controlled experiments with the goal of unravelling the secret behind his method. The outcome of one of these experiments showed that when applying the method, regions in the periaqueductal grey part of the brain were activated. This is the part of the brain that is the primary control centre for pain suppression. This is a promising discovery that could lead to a potential role for the WHM as an endogenous painkiller and reflects results we already see in people who effectively use the WHM to combat their conditions.

There is a lot of the scientific research on his website about how the program affects the amygdala, but what is important here are his results. If you want to read more about brain responses, you can look at his website.

In one of his experiments, students of the WHM were able to control their sympathetic nervous systems and their immune responses while they were injected with an endotoxin. Trained participants showed fewer symptoms, lower levels of proinflammatory mediators, and increased levels of plasma epinephrine (adrenaline). This could mean that the WHM may be an effective tool in battling symptoms of various autoimmune diseases.

He found that after just a few weeks, people started to experience benefits that included better sleep, more energy, less stress, improved focus, and a better mood. I started turning down the hot water and ending my showers with cold water for a few minutes in summer. I experienced more energy, less pain, and better sleep. Some of my clients have reported feeling less anxiety.

Hof demonstrates everything you need to know about following his method, including breathing exercises, meditation, and cold training on his website. The web address is in the Resources section.

Chapter 7

Medication

Medication does help some people, and I would never tell people what to do in that department. I'm not a doctor. However, many of the people I see are adamant that they don't want medication. And in many cases, they don't need them. That discussion needs to be with their doctors.

There are alternative ways of looking at depression and anxiety. What if the modern way of understanding depression and anxiety is wrong? I read recently an extract titled *Is Everything You Think You Know about Depression Wrong?* about a book called *Lost Connections: Uncovering the Real Causes of Depression—and the Unexpected Solutions"* by British writer Johann Hari. I started to see depression and anxiety in a different way. In it, Hari explains that sometimes what we're feeling is not a chemical imbalance in the brain but a reaction to something that is happening in our lives. A normal reaction considering that circumstance.

In Hari's book, he relates research that he carried out and the many experts he consulted. He determined that in Western medicine since the 1970s, doctors were taught in medical school that depression is

33

a chemical imbalance in the brain, a dangerous thing, therefore a disease that needs medication. I have found sometimes there is an imbalance.

But I have had clients who believed that everything was good in their lives but still felt bad. However, with most clients, we find a reason for their depression, such as grief. Depression can also be unexpressed anger or anger turned inwards.

Hari also discusses grief. People who are experiencing grief have identical symptoms to someone who is depressed. But feeling grief is normal and natural; it will decrease in time without antidepressants. Dr. Joanne Cacciatore, associate professor at Arizona State University, is a leading expert on grief. In his book, Hari reveals her perspective:

> She told me this debate reveals a key problem with how we talk about depression, anxiety and other forms of suffering: we don't, she said, "consider context". We act like human distress can be assessed solely on a checklist that can be separated out from our lives, and labelled as brain diseases. If we started to take people's actual lives into account when we treat depression and anxiety ... it would require "an entire system overhaul" ... when "you have a person with extreme human distress, [we need to] stop treating the symptoms. The symptoms are a messenger of a deeper problem. Let's get to the deeper problem.

Hari was a teenager when he became depressed. When he finally found the courage to consult a doctor, he was told that he had a serotonin imbalance, a faulty brain, and that medication would make him feel normal again. The problem with medication is that our bodies can become used to it. and when it doesn't work as well, we have to increase the dose or change to a different medication. This does not even question whether there is an underlying reason for the way one feels. Hari found that after some time, the emotional pain came back.

He started his research to answer two questions for himself. Why was he feeling so bad when he was doing everything he had been told to do? And why were there so many other people feeling the same way? The number of people being medicated for depression and anxiety was growing alarmingly throughout the first world. Surely that many people's brains couldn't be malfunctioning at the same time, and if they were, why?

Hari embarked on a journey around the world, talking to leading scientists and asking them the questions above. He also spoke with people who overcame depression in unexpected ways, including an Amish village in Indiana, a Brazilian city that banned advertising, and a laboratory in Baltimore. From these people he learned there are many natural causes of depression and anxiety. He found there evidence that seven specific factors in the way we are living today can cause depression and anxiety to increase. These can combine with environmental factors (such as the people you associate with) to make depression and anxiety worse.

Researching his book, he discovered that up to 80 percent of people who were prescribed antidepressants were depressed again within a year as their bodies became used to the medications which then no longer functioned as well. He believed, as do I, that we also need to consider alternative therapies.

His book questions the belief that depression is caused only by a spontaneous lowering of serotonin. Hari found scientific and anecdotal evidence that it can also be caused by environmental or situational factors, or long-term depressed thought patterns. His research, and that of many other social scientists, found that the majority of people have genuine reasons for their depression, many of which relate to a feeling of lack of control over their lives. Reasons which can include hating their work or life situations, long-term financial stress, or chronic pain. The full article is well worth reading, and the web address is in the Resources section.

Also highlighting lack of control is a recent article by Sarah Berger on CNBC, "Dr. Oz: This Is the Best Thing You Can Do for Your Mental Health in 2019". In it, Dr. Mehmet Oz says, "The best thing you can do ... to create the mental health you want and deserve is to be proactive in your life ... So, decide what you want to do, and just go after it. [Don't be] abrasive or aggressive, it just means that you have to feel like you control your destiny."

This feeling of control can begin by creating easy habits, which include you deciding when you go to sleep at night and what time you wake up in the morning. This, he says, can have a profound impact on your mental health. Oz explains that during sleep, our brain cells shrink a little bit to allow the channels in between them to freely clean out toxins, "to sort of reboot the brain every evening."

Oz advocates that we do "the appropriate work" by creating meaningful, helpful habits. These include quality sleep, meditation, eating healthily—that is, foods that we know stimulate our brain—avoiding toxins that we know pull away thought focus, and not getting distracted by things that don't really apply to our desired life path. The address for this article is in the Resources section.

Chapter 8

Motivation

Many depressed and anxious people have problems with motivation. They want to do the things they need to do to help themselves but can't make themselves do It. In my experience, and as Louise L. Hay stated in her *12 Ways to Love Yourself,* it is not helpful to beat yourself up when you're not living up to your expectations. This only makes you feel worse and want to go to bed, pull the blankets over your head, and hide from the world. Been there.

Writing a to-do list can be a good start. Don't get carried away and write too many things on your list. That will only overwhelm you, and you are back to just going to bed again. Limit your list to three to five things in order of importance. If you're very depressed, it may be, 1. Get out of bed, 2. Brush your teeth, 3. Have a shower. If you do the things on your list, cross them off. Crossing things off a list gives a feeling of accomplishment which can create more dopamine (the happy hormone) in your brain.

Completing the items on your list can also help create what psychologists call an internal locus of control, which means that you believe you are the master of your life. That you are able to control how your life goes. An example that I used in my degree thesis, which studied locus of control, was, if you were walking down the street and tripped over an uneven piece of footpath, would you think, *I'll be more careful next time, and that won't happen again,* or, *The Council should take better care of the footpath. I'm not safe to walk along here.*

If you thought the first thought, you have an internal locus of control; you believe you can control what happens to you. If you had the second thought, you would have an external locus of control, meaning that you believe outside forces make things happen to you, and you cannot control what happens to you. People with an external locus of control have a victim mentality which causes them to be less likely to be motivated. They have more thoughts of *It's their fault. I can't do anything to help myself, so why bother? It won't make any difference anyway.* This thinking leads to depression and then anxiety.

I encourage my clients to watch a useful clip featuring Mel Robbins outlining her "5-second rule" of motivation that she formulated from her own life. "If you have an impulse to act on a goal, you must physically move within 5 seconds or your brain will kill the idea." This built her internal locus of control and helped her to become more motivated the more often it worked. The address for this clip is in the Resources section. Mel Robbins also has other very good clips, resources and books.

Another technique I learned from a book on organising is to trick yourself into things. Something that worked well for me when my children were young and I was a stay-at-home mother was to clean in short bursts. The book recommended that if a room, such as the kitchen, needed cleaning, put the kettle on to make a cup of tea or coffee, and while it boils, race yourself to do as much as you can. When it boils, make your drink, sit down, and drink it. I drank lots of tea over the day, so this strategy worked very well for me. By the time I made a few cups of tea, the kitchen was so much tidier that I didn't have any trouble finishing the job.

The same book also recommended that instead of deciding to do a big purge and then never getting around to it, keep some bags or boxes in your bedroom. Then, when you see something that needs to go to charity or be given to someone, put it into the appropriate box or bag. When the charity box is full, donate the contents. Or when you see the person to whom you wish to give something, you know where to find it.

Another tip that worked for me was to use containers and organisation. If you have a quickly accessible place for everything, it makes it easier to tidy and find things next time. Think of a kindergarten or childcare centre. A place for everything and everything in its place. Once you get used to it, it makes life easier.

Chapter 9

Affirmations and Goals

Some people believe in affirmations, some don't, and some prefer to call them SMART goals. SMART is an acronym which stands for specific, measurable, attainable, relevant, and time-able. "Specific" means including lots of details; don't be wishy-washy. I heard a story; not sure if it's true, but you don't want to take chances. A woman wrote a goal stating that she would lose a certain number of kilograms by a particular date. She had a freak boating accident and lost her leg which was the exact number of kilogramss that she wanted to lose. Be specific about what, how, why, and when.

"Measurable" means you can gauge when you achieve it. When I talk to people about their SMART goals, they often say they want to be happy or have more free time. How would you know if you were happy? Would you be smiling more? I often recommend contentment instead; that is more stable. You can be happy about something, but that comes and goes. You can be content even when your happiness quota goes up or down. How much more free time do you want? You could find yourself suddenly with no job. Voila, you have more free time. The reticular activating system in your brain helps to actuate your goals and needs a lot of specific data to go on.

"Attainable" means it needs to be achievable. I would like to be taller, but it doesn't matter how many SMART goals I write, I don't think that can happen. You must believe it can happen in the time frame you have set. You can write, "I'm going to receive a million dollars a month from now," but if your subconscious doesn't believe you can, it won't happen.

The subconscious mind is far more powerful than the conscious mind. I often use the analogy of a ship. The conscious mind is like the captain of a ship, with his maps and compass. He looks at his map and decides to go north. However, it doesn't matter how much the captain wants to go north if the subconscious mind, which is like the ship's engine, remembers a past event where going north was dangerous. It will make sure that the ship doesn't go north. Before we understand why this happens, we can punish ourselves severely by believing we are lazy, unmotivated, or stupid.

"Relevant' refers to the focus of the goal. Is it relevant to your life? If you haven't done the courses to qualify for a particular job, it doesn't do any good to write a SMART goal to get that as your perfect job. You need to start with taking the first step to achieving what you want.

"Time-able" refers to the date you want this outcome to manifest. I often recommend monthly goals. If you want an outcome in one month but don't write down the date, the subconscious thinks there is no hurry, and you may only get it in six years. To work fully, the subconscious needs as much information as it can get. All this information goes to the reticular activating system to help you achieve your goals.

The reticular activating system is an automatic goal-seeking mechanism often known as RAS. The RAS plays a vital role in one's ability to achieve goals. The brain is busy thinking all the time. Scientists estimate that we have approximately sixty thousand thoughts every day, and about 90 percent of them are the same thoughts we had yesterday. Sixty thousand thoughts are too many to fit into the conscious part of our brains, which is much smaller than the subconscious part of our brain.

About 75 percent of our thoughts go straight through to the subconscious without us even realising we have had them. Part of the job of the RAS is to take notice of those thoughts and make sure that the important ones to you, preferences, health factors, and safety factors are taken notice of. Any thoughts that aren't of immediate importance are filtered straight to the subconscious, where they are filed for if they are needed.

An example that most people can relate to is when you, or someone you know, gets a new car, and you have never noticed that make, model, or colour before. Once you do, you start to notice them more and more. Where did they come from? They were always there; you just didn't notice them. Another example is even in a noisy room, you will notice someone say your name, or a mother will hear her child cry. That's the RAS functioning.

The RAS is what starts SMART goals or affirmations working. When you write down your goal or affirmation, start repeating it to yourself often, feeling the emotion of it. Because your brain remembers highly emotional thoughts or events, the RAS will take notice, and you will start to see evidence of what you want. Your mind wants to give you whatever you want. You just have to prime it in the right way.

The RAS is always trying to assist us by helping us notice things. The problem is with the way it decides what you want to see; it listens to our thoughts from the last few days and weeks. If they have been negative, depressed, or anxious thoughts, it decides that is what you want. Therefore, it finds all those thoughts and makes sure you notice them. That is why when we are in a negative mood, ten good things could happen and one bad thing, but we can't stop focusing on that one bad thing. There is a saying in psychology: "What we focus on grows in our attention."

Below are some examples of affirmations I have said often and which have become true for me. I left off the dates in most of them because they are ones I want to continue.

Health

I am so happy; my life and health are getting better and better. I am meditating and exercising for half an hour every day. I eat healthy food, drink lemon water, and take my supplements. I'm sleeping well every night. I have wonderful health in mind and body.

Mental Health

I am enjoying helping people every day. I have lots of energy. I give every-one lots of value. The business is growing all the time, and we are helping more people, bringing more abundance, health, and love to everyone involved for the highest good of all concerned.

Passion

I am enjoying living my passion, working on my book and notes every week. My book is published and selling by the end of the year. It is helping more and more people, more than I could believe.

Relationship

My husband and I, the kids, and grandkids are getting closer and having great family experiences often. I have balance in my life. I love and accept myself just as I am, and that spreads to my extended family. I have wonderful friends, I enjoy spending time with them often.

Spiritual

I read and learn all the time. I journal, prioritize my next day, meditate, and pray every day. I see things to be grateful for every day.

There is an even more scientific explanation related to quantum psychics as to why affirmations can work in the next chapter.

Chapter 10

The Wonderful World of Quantum Physics

I recently watched an interesting talk by Dr. Joe Dispenza called "How to Unlock the Full Potential of Your Mind". In it, he explained in a very easy to understand way that our negative thoughts get stuck in a loop which then causes more anxiety thoughts to form in your brain.

Dispenza explains how thought patterns are wired into your brain through synaptic firing. "Neurons that fire together wire together." (nuralplasticity) If you wake up in the morning and start remembering all the things that are wrong in your life, all the negative things that have happened, or negative encounters that you have had, your brain doesn't know they are just memories; it starts reliving the memories as if they are happening right now. We can feel upset all over again simply by remembering how we felt in the past. When this happens, we are priming how we will feel today. This becomes the program that runs our lives, and we are set to be negative people who discount anything positive that happens and perceive anything negative that happens as what was only to be expected. This can lead to further depression and anxiety.

This is a subconscious program that we don't even realise we are running until we start to become more conscious of the sixty thousand plus thoughts that flit through our brains every day. When we become conscious of our negative thoughts, we can decide what we want to think. As mentioned before, we can change our limiting self-beliefs in a conscious way through repetition and neuroplasticity, SMART goals, hypnosis, or meditation.

Dispenza recommends that "meditation [is] a tool we can use to change those emotions that keep us in the familiar past." He states that practising meditation helps to get beyond the analytical mind which separates the conscious mind from the subconscious mind. Through practice, we can change our brainwaves, slow them down. And when we do that properly, we can make some really important changes.

He mentions the Newtonian world (Isaac Newton's beliefs of how the world worked) as, "the old model of reality … of cause and effect … Waiting for something outside of us to change how we feel inside of us. The Newtonian World is all about the predictable. It's all about predicting the future."

He goes on to say that "the Quantum Model of Reality is about causing the effect … The moment you start feeling whole your healing begins … and when you love yourself and you love … life you're causing an effect." In other words, your subjective mind has an effect on your objective world.

There is a fascinating article by Philip Ball "The Strange Link between the Human Mind and Quantum Physics" on the BBC website that is well worth reading. The web address is in the Resources section.

Another fascinating article is by Julie Beck in the magazine *The Atlantic*. In her article, "How 'Quantum Cognition' Can Explain Humans' Irrational Behaviors", she draws on research from a pair of studies from the Ohio State University, Indiana University, and the Queensland University of Technology, as well as Jerome Busemeyer and Peter Bruza's book *Quantum Models of Cognition and Decision* to explain quantum cognition. This new theory posits that the mathematical principles behind quantum mechanics can be used to better understand human behaviour. The web address is in the Resources section.

I often talk to clients when they first start really listening to their thoughts. When they begin to notice how often they think negative thoughts, I counsel them not to beat themselves up for having such thoughts. They need to recognise those thoughts for what they are and move forward. If instead of, *Damn, I'm thinking that thought again,* you think, *Great, now I can go back to what I do want* and repeat the desired thought to yourself five times every time you think the original thought, the second thought will eventually be stronger. This is neuroplasticity at work.

Chapter 11

Boundaries

This chapter is about parenting. However, it is good to know our values and develop positive boundaries in all our relationships. The more positively assertive you are in your interactions, the less confusing and better your relationships are. This can help you to have higher self-esteem and internal locus of control as you feel more in control of your relationships.

The Perils of Parenting

Having different views than your partner when it comes to parenting is a stressful way to live. It is confusing for the children in your family too. They find it hard to know which parent to listen to and how to avoid getting into trouble. They will often just go with the most aggressive parent. It is very disempowering to have a partner countermand or disregard your rules in front of the children. There will be times when you do disagree, but try to do that behind closed doors and present a united front to the children.

Parenting 101

Parenting is hard work, and everyone has an opinion. This does not make anyone right or wrong. Following are some insights I have learned over the years. I hope they may clarify some issues and make sense to you. Use what you like, and disregard the rest.

Boundaries

It's hard teaching children to follow rules and learn right from wrong. Mostly they learn by example from their parents. For example, trying to stop your child from swearing when you do it in front of him or her is impossible and confusing for the child. From day 1 you are your children's first boundary, and they need to know they are safe with you.

Think of the analogy of a roller coaster. Life is scary and has many ups and downs. When you go on a roller coaster, the assistant locks you in with seat belts, and the first thing you do is test them to see if they hold. That's what children are doing when they test your boundaries and rules. On a subconscious level, they know they shouldn't be in charge; they feel more secure if the boundaries hold. On a conscious level, they may yell, cry, and have tantrums. But in the long run, they will feel secure knowing the boundaries hold. It takes an average of six weeks before they believe you are serious about being consistent, and then life settles down for a while. They will test again every so often to see if you are still in charge. Stay consistent. Following are some strategies I have found effective.

Consequences 101

1. With your partner, or by yourself if you are single, decide what is important to you and what is not. It is best to have fewer rules and stick to them consistently than to have lots that you don't enforce when you're tired, stressed, or feel guilty. Consistency is crucial. Rules changing depending on the day and how the parent feels confuse children and make them insecure. "If my parents can't make up their minds and don't know what they're doing, who does?"

2. Decide what the consequences will be for each problem. The consequences don't have to be huge or painful. They just need to be consistent and age appropriate. The rule of thumb for time out is one minute for each year of age. For example, a two-year-old gets two minutes of time out. For older children, you can use the withdrawal of TV, internet, or games with appropriate times, half an hour to start with. You may need to use it more than a few times in one day. If you have already taken away the game for the whole day, what next?

3. Sit down in a family meeting and discuss with your children how boundaries help the family get along together and make family life and relationships more harmonious. You can write the rules and the consequences on a large sheet of paper, even laminate it. Pictures can help children who can't read.

4. When they test you—and they will—remain cool, calm, and collected. Point to the chart and remind them what was discussed and agreed on. Give them one more chance to do what was agreed on. Praise goes a long way when they are doing the right thing. If they don't, calmly enforce the consequence.

5. Any self-respecting child will object, complain, and even have a tantrum. That's okay, remain calm. Depending on

the age of the child and the situation, you can walk away, change the subject, or stay there to enforce the consequence. You can validate the child's feelings by saying such things as, "Yes, I can see you're angry and frustrated," or, "I know you're sad that you can't have it," or remind them, "Next time, you'll behave differently, and this won't have to happen." Put the cause back on them. They chose the behaviour, therefore they chose the consequence. It's that simple.

6. Finally, it is important to distinguish between the child and the behaviour. We can not like the behaviour while still loving and liking the child. Also, when a child says, "I don't like you," or, "I hate you," remember that it is the situation they don't like. They still love you. I used to say to my children, "It's okay to feel like that right now. I still love you." It's useful to talk to a friend or therapist to get support when things get tough.

Another strategy I have found that works is a magical question that can be asked of children as they get older. Children learn resilience when they learn that they can control their emotions and solve their own problems. We need to help them think and figure out what is happening to and for them. Firstly, they need their feelings validated and acknowledged. In a calm voice ask, "Are you frustrated or angry because you can't have xyz? Then the magical question that can make them stop and think. They have to have some maturity for this. Get the child's attention, look him or her in the eye, and ask calmly, "Is this a big problem, a medium problem, or a small problem? How should we fix it?" When we acknowledge what they are going through, and at the same time make them participate in solving the problem, we can disarm the tantrum and give them the confidence that they can be in control of themselves.

Every time you ask the question and your child answers, and you find a way to solve the problem—starting from the perception of where to look for the solution—it builds on the last time. A small problem is always quick and simple to solve. There are some problems they will consider medium. They will most likely be solved, but not at that instant. And the child will have to understand there are things that need some time to happen. If a problem is serious from the child's point of view, it is important that it's not dismissed, even though it may seem silly to us. You might need to talk it over further, and help your child understand that sometimes there are things that do not go exactly the way we want.

An example of this magic question being used recently was when one of my clients was choosing clothes for school with her daughter. The daughter often makes a big fuss over her outfits, especially when the weather is cooler. To summarize, she wanted to wear her favourite dress, but it was in the wash. She started to melt down, and my client asked, "Is this a big, medium, or small problem?" Her daughter looked up sheepishly and said quietly, "Small." Then my client once again explained that they already knew that small problems are easy to solve. She asked for her suggestions on how they could solve that small problem. She had learned that it is important to give her time to think and respond. Her daughter replied, "Choosing another dress." My client added, "And you have more than one dress to choose from." She smiled and went to get another dress. My client congratulated her on having solved the problem herself. Tantrum averted.

Good luck, and happy parenting.

Chapter 12

Meditation

Meditation has been researched extensively, including the Maharishi Effect. An example of which is an Indian study which analysed the impact on the crime rate in New Delhi of a group of meditation experts attending a course there from November 1980 to April 1981. The impact of the group was assessed using daily crime totals from June 1980 to March 1981. After all cycles and trends were removed, the estimated impact of the group was highly statistically significant, showing an 11 percent decrease in the crime rate. Similar results have been reported in Merseyside in the United Kingdom, and Washington, DC in the United States.

As I have discussed meditation so often in this book, and it has been recommended by so many learned people, I thought it would be useful to end this book with a meditation that I wrote myself. You could record yourself saying it. Or if you don't think you would listen to yourself, a version is available on freemindspsychology. com.au.

Find a quiet, comfortable place to relax where you won't be disturbed, and make sure you are comfortable. Feel free to move anytime you have a need to. It's better to move than to be focused on a pain or an itch. During this meditation, I talk sometimes and am quiet at other times, so you can visualise and practice being in the present moment.

I encourage you through this meditation to focus on your energy and project it to other people or groups. So ...

Sit or lie with your eyes closed, and concentrate on your breathing, making it slow and even ... in ... 2 ... 3 ... 4, and out ... 2 ... 3 ... 4. Try to allow your breathing to stay slow and even while concentrating on my voice. If you get distracted, don't stress because it is very common. Research shows the average brain gets distracted every six seconds. Just notice with interest and compassion, and start counting your breaths again to bring you back to the present moment.

Now I want you to imagine yourself sitting or lying in a safe, peaceful, beautiful place ... the most peaceful safe place you can imagine. This is your own private place. And while you are in this place ... right this moment, everything is right with the world ... You are relaxed and comfortable ... there is nothing you need to do, nowhere you need to be ... and everyone you love and care about is okay ... Right this minute, everything is okay.

Because this is your private place, you are perfectly safe ... and no one can come into this place unless you invite them. ...

You start to notice how calm ... relaxed ... peaceful, and content you feel ... just relaxing in this time and place, just breathing ... more relaxed and content than you've been in a long time. All your muscles are relaxing, and you feel as if you are sinking comfortably into the chair or floor ...

Imagine the relaxation flowing down and around your body like a gentle mist or soft silk … starting at the top of your head. Relax your forehead, your eyes, your jaw; we hold lots of tension in our jaws. You may want to move your jaw to release the tension. Your neck and shoulders may have tension as well.

Feel the relaxation flowing down over your shoulders … down your arms … to your fingertips … down your torso … Feel your diaphragm moving in and out with your breath. This relaxed feeling continues down your legs … ankles … and feet.

You now notice some inviting stone stairs going downwards. You feel safe and drawn to go down these stairs … Imagine yourself at the top of the stairs, watching your feet going down each step, and feeling more deeply relaxed, content, peaceful, and safe with each step you take. They lead you to the most relaxing, safe place you can imagine. It may be a garden, a forest, or even a beach … wherever you feel most relaxed. You notice a comfortable chair or couch to sit or lie on. You relax into it and feel like you are melting into the furniture. And you feel grounded into the earth. Your in-breath is coming all the way from deep in the earth, and you can feel it entering your body and going through your limbs all the way to your fingers and toes. Then, as it leaves your body, imagine your breath taking all the toxins and negativity out with each breath. Imagine all the toxins and negativity becoming a big ball of black mist you send out into the air to be neutralized. Continue doing this until you feel like your body has been cleansed and is peaceful.

Now, imagine drawing into your heart all the loving energy you can hold. Feel this energy fill every part of your body. When you are completely full, imagine sending this energy to other people in your home, family, or community. See the loving energy as a light, bright mist surrounding these people, and the energy helping them in their days. Take a few minutes to send this energy.

Whenever we hold onto negative feelings towards another person, it affects us more than it affects them. I encourage you to start with smaller, easier negative feelings. Picture someone with whom you are irritated, and regardless of fault or blame, send them loving, forgiving energy. Picture them standing before you, and let go of all negative thoughts and feelings so that you feel more peaceful and centred.

We are all energy vibrating at a different frequencies, and our frequency can change with our emotions. One of the highest frequencies is gratitude. We can cultivate an attitude or habit of gratitude by practicing feeling gratitude.

For the next few minutes, bring to mind between five and ten things that you could be grateful for from the last twenty-four hours. It can be something small, such as, "I had a nice dinner last night," or, "I have a safe, comfortable bed to sleep in." Or perhaps someone did something kind for you. This practice raises our vibrations, helps us feel better in the present moment, and helps us notice positive things that happen in our lives more often.

The next part of the meditation is to project yourself two years into the future. Imagine how you would like your life to be in two years. Who do you want in your life? What are you doing with your life? What are your health and body like? What do you do for fun? Your thoughts, when you think them enough, become goals. If we focus on them enough, they manifest in the real world.

Now, I want you to picture your perfect day that would help make your future vision come into reality. How would your perfect day go? Do you feel fantastic and exited to wake up and spring out of bed? Imagine having a delicious, healthy breakfast … working at your perfect job … enjoying your day … interacting with people you respect, care about, or love. Having a great dinner with a person or people you love. A peaceful evening and a good, refreshing sleep, knowing that this day will bring you to your perfect life.

Take a last look around your safe place. Memorize how it looks and feels so that you can come back to this place at any time. Anytime it is safe and appropriate to sit or lie for even a few minutes, you can take yourself back to your safe place and enjoy the benefits of your meditation.

When you have finished memorizing your safe place, we come out of the meditation feeling positive ... refreshed ... ready to make your day the best day that you can have today. As I count backward from five, you will come back to the room feeling positive, rejuvenated, and looking forward to the rest of today and tomorrow: 5, 4, 3, 2, 1 ... Welcome back.

Each time you do this meditation, or a version of it, it becomes easier. Our bodies have muscle memory, so each time becomes easier as our bodies remember what relaxation, peace, and calm feel like.

Conclusion

In conclusion, this book is full of information from many wonderful, intelligent people from many walks of life and who have many different ideas. I have tried to compile information that I and the people I've helped have found useful. It is my greatest wish that you have found some things in this book that help make your life better, easier, and more stable. As Dr. Daniel Amen advocates, helping one person can also help that person's immediate family and, in turn, their descendants as they will be guided by someone who is more stable, wise, and happy.

Resources

My Website

freemindspsychology.com.au
Facebook Free Minds Psychology

Web Links

Dr. Daniel Amen
https://www.amenclinics.com/blog/12-prescriptions-for-creating-a-brain-healthy-life-part-1/https://www.amenclinics.com/blog/12-prescriptions-creating-brain-healthy-life-part-2/

Dr. Scot N. Bay
https://holisticprimarycare.net/topics/topics-o-z/psyche-some-a-spirit/1937-do-probiotics-have-a-first-line-role-in-depression-treatment.html

Jack Canfield
https://www.jackcanfield.com

Dr. Joe Dispenza
https://www.youtube.com/watch?v=1PPaw-INs3Q (*Interview with Dispenza commences at 1:30 in the video)*

Louise L. Hay
https://www.healyourlife.com/
how-to-love-yourself-now-in-12-easy-ways

Wim Hof
https://www.wimhofmethod.com/

Marisa Peer
The Biggest Disease Affecting Humanity: "I'm Not Enough"
https://www.youtube.com/watch?v=lw3NyUMLh7Y

Dr. John E. Sarno
https://www.johnesarnomd.com/

TSM Help Forum
http://rsi-backpain.co.uk/how-to-cure-tms/

<u>TEDx TALKS</u>

Dr. Shawn Achor
"The Happiness Advantage: Linking Positive Brains to Performance"
TEDxBloomington
https://www.youtube.com/watch?v=GXy__kBVq1M

Dr. Daniel Amen
"Change Your Brain, Change Your Life"
TEDxOrangeCoast
https://www.youtube.com/watch?v=MLKj1puoWCg"Beautiful Minds"
TEDxOrangeCoast
https://www.youtube.com/watch?v=esPRsT-lmw8

Dr. Joe Dispenza

TEDx Tacoma
"How to Unlock the Full Potential of Your Mind"
https://www.youtube.com/watch?v=La9oLLoI5Rc

Dr. Sara Lazar
"How Meditation Can Reshape Our Brains"
TEDxCambridge 2011
https://www.youtube.com/watch?v=m8rRzTtP7Tc

Mel Robbins
"How to Stop Screwing Yourself Over"
TEDxSF https://www.youtube.com/
watch?v=Lp7E973zozc&feature=youtu.be

ARTICLES

Johann Hari
Is Everything You Think You Know About Depression Wrong?
https://www.theguardian.com/society/2018/jan/07/is-everything-you-think-you-know-about-depression-wrong-johann-hari-lost-connections

Philip Ball
"The Strange Link between the Human Mind and Quantum Physics."
www.bbc.com/earth/story/20170215-the-strange-link-between-the-human-mind-and-quantum-physics

Julie Beck
"How 'Quantum Cognition' Can Explain Humans' Irrational Behaviors"
https://www.theatlantic.com/health/archive/2015/09/how-quantum-cognition-can-explain-humans-irrational-behaviors/405787/

Amanda Brewer, B. Beh Sc (Phych).

Sarah Berger
"Dr. Oz: This Is the Best Thing You Can Do for Your Mental Health in 2019—and It's Free."
https://www.cnbc.com/2018/12/20/dr-oz-this-is-the-best-thing-you-can-do-for-your-mental-health.html?recirc=taboolainternal

The Maharishi Effect
Dillbeck, M. C., Cavanaugh, K. L., Glenn, T., Orme-Johnson, D. W., & Mittlefehldt, V. (1987). "Consciousness as a field: The Transcendental Meditation and TM-Sidhi program and changes in social indicators." *The Journal of Mind and Behavior*, 8(1), 67–104.
Quoted in "Summary of 13 Maharishi Effect Published Studies," https://research.mum.edu/maharishi-effect/summary-of-13-published-studies.

Printed in the United States
By Bookmasters